MW01489135

*GREATER TH.
ALSO AVAILABLE IN EBOOK AND
AUDIOBOOK FORMAT.

Greater Than a Tourist
Book Series
Reviews from Readers

Good information to have to plan my trip to this destination.

-Pennie Farrell, Mexico

Great ideas for a port day.

-Mary Martin USA

Aptly titled, you won't just be a tourist after reading this book. You'll be greater than a tourist!

-Alan Warner, Grand Rapids, USA

Even though I only have three days to spend in San Miguel in an upcoming visit, I will use the author's suggestions to guide some of my time there. An easy read - with chapters named to guide me in directions I want to go.

-Robert Catapano, USA

Great insights from a local perspective! Useful information and a very good value!

-Sarah, USA

This series provides an in-depth experience through the eyes of a local. Reading these series will help you to travel the city in with confidence and it'll make your journey a unique one.

-Andrew Teoh, Ipoh, Malaysia

GREATER THAN A TOURIST- ABACO ISLANDS BAHAMAS

50 Travel Tips from a Local

Vueendra Rolle

CZYK Publishing Since 2011.
CZYKPublishing.com
Greater Than a Tourist

Lock Haven, PA
All rights reserved.

>TOURIST

50 TRAVEL TIPS FROM A LOCAL

BOOK DESCRIPTION

With travel tips and culture in our guidebooks written by a local, it is never too late to visit the Abaco Islands. Greater than a tourist - Abaco, Bahamas by Vueendra Rolle offers the inside scoop on the Boatman's dream Island and its cays.

Most travel books tell you how to travel like a tourist. Although there is nothing wrong with that, as part of the 'Greater Than a Tourist' series, this book will give you candid travel tips from someone who has lived at your next travel destination. This guide book will not tell you exact addresses or store hours but instead gives you knowledge that you may not find in other smaller print travel books. Experience cultural, culinary delights, and attractions with the guidance of a Local. Slow down and get to know the people with this invaluable guide. By the time you finish this book, you will be eager and prepared to discover new activities at your next travel destination.

Inside this travel guide book you will find:

Visitor information from a Local
Tour ideas and inspiration
Save time with valuable guidebook information

Greater Than a Tourist- A Travel Guidebook with 50 Travel Tips from a Local. Slow down, stay in one place, and get to know the people and culture. By the time you finish this book, you will be eager and prepared to travel to your next destination.

OUR STORY

Traveling is a passion of the Greater than a Tourist book series creator. Lisa studied abroad in college, and for their honeymoon Lisa and her husband toured Europe. During her travels to Malta, an older man tried to give her some advice based on his own experience living on the island since he was a young boy. She was not sure if she should talk to the stranger but was interested in his advice. When traveling to some places she was wary to talk to locals because she was afraid that they weren't being genuine. Through her travels, Lisa learned how much locals had to share with tourists. Lisa created the Greater Than a Tourist book series to help connect people with locals. A topic that locals are very passionate about sharing.

TABLE OF CONTENTS

DEDICATION

This book is dedicated to the people of Abaco for their unwavering resilience and determination.

ABOUT THE AUTHOR

Vueendra Rolle is a young local that lives on the beautiful island of Abaco. She loves reading, relaxing by the water, writing, and new experiences. She has resided in Abaco for over twenty years enduring the hardships that came with the latest hurricane in 2019 that nearly wiped the island clean of homes, shops, hotels, etc. Luckily like most of the locals on the island, she managed to rebuild her life again stronger than ever.

HOW TO USE THIS BOOK

The *Greater Than a Tourist* book series was written by someone who has lived in an area for over three months. The goal of this book is to help travelers either dream or experience different locations by providing opinions from a local. The author has made suggestions based on their own experiences. Please check before traveling to the area in case the suggested places are unavailable.

Travel Advisories: As a first step in planning any trip abroad, check the Travel Advisories for your intended destination.
https://travel.state.gov/content/travel/en/traveladvisories/traveladvisories.html

FROM THE PUBLISHER

Traveling can be one of the most important parts of a person's life. The anticipation and memories that you have are some of the best. As a publisher of the Greater Than a Tourist, as well as the popular *50 Things to Know* book series, we strive to help you learn about new places, spark your imagination, and inspire you. Wherever you are and whatever you do I wish you safe, fun, and inspiring travel.

Lisa Rusczyk Ed. D.
CZYK Publishing

WELCOME TO
> TOURIST

I have a place that I go to in The Bahamas. It's the only place that guarantees total anonymity and freedom.

-Johnny Depp

A baco is indeed a joyous little island where one can be completely free.The people and the atmosphere are warm and inviting. In fact, we are generally known for our hospitality to others. Hospitality aside, I believe the best attribute of Abaco is the delicious local food. One taste and you will want to go back home with recipes.

If you are interested in planning a trip to Abaco and don't know where to start then don't fret. I will give you some advice and recommendations to help you from planning to the actual experience. I will also tell you about a few of my experiences.

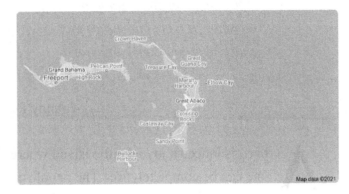

Great Abaco

The Bahamas

Abaco Islands Bahamas Climate

	High	Low
January	77	66
February	77	65
March	78	67
April	81	69
May	82	70
June	82	70
July	87	75
August	88	76
September	88	75
October	84	74
November	81	71
December	79	67

GreaterThanaTourist.com

Temperatures are in Fahrenheit degrees.
Source: NOAA

1. LET'S GET TECHNICAL

First and foremost before you go anywhere you must know where you are going. When people hear the word Abaco they usually think of one island however, it's not. To be technically correct, think of it as a three-piece puzzle. It is divided into Mainland which is also called Great Abaco, outer land is also known as Little Abaco, and its Cays.

Each of these areas is separated by water; however, Great Abaco and Little Abaco are connected by a bridge. If you need to get to a Cay you will have to travel by ferry. Knowing exactly where you are going to stay beforehand is beneficial especially with time management. While I am on the topic of time management, let me give you some estimates of traveling time in Abaco.

- From the main airport in Marsh Harbour (Leonard M. Thompson International Airport) to Little Abaco takes about two hours.
- From A Cay to Little Abaco is about one hour.
- Marsh Harbour to Sandy Point is about two hours give or take.

2. MAKE ARRANGEMENTS

Vacations should be fun and hassle-free in my opinion. So instead of trying to run around like a chicken without a head trying to get things together after you've arrived in Abaco; try making arrangements and booking earlier. Make those calls, book that hotel reservation, secure your ferry tickets. I suggest booking plane tickets a month before for the best prices. It will help you in making sure things go right. Make the most out of your time and save yourself the stress. The less time you spend worrying about arrangements the more time you have to relax and enjoy your time in Abaco. That said, I will just give you a few Ferry names for you to find their current website since they are subject to change with time.

- Green Turtle Cay ferry
- The ferry at the crossing
- Treasure Cay Airport ferry terminal
- Albury's Ferry
- The ferry ltd

3. PACKING FOR AN ISLAND VACAY

Now that we have already made your arrangements, it's time to get down to packing. When packing for a vacation to Abaco the main thing I would say is a must to bring is sunscreen. Sure you've heard it a million times already but it is essential to have. I'm sure you've heard of the extremely hot weather of The Bahamas and let me confirm it's no joke. The last time I went to the beach I was sunburnt for weeks. So don't learn the hard way kids, bring sunscreen especially if you're planning to soak up sunlight on the beach.

Next, we have slippers. They are easy to travel in and are very lightweight. They help with walking on the beach and around in general. Since it's very hot here sneakers wouldn't be the best choice so go for something comfortable. The next thing to bring of course is clothes. However since this is Abaco, dressing here is based on the fact that the sun loves us so dearly. Nevertheless, I can say a sundress is a go-to for women (this is fitting considering the circumstances) and shorts will do nicely for males.

Another helpful item is insect repellent. Since it is an island with lots of trees and bushes mosquitoes are bound to take up residency here. Help yourself and just avoid those little stinging insects. Finally, we have a travel day pack for your daily belongings if you go out on a little adventure or even if you just want to go to the beach.

4. CURRENCY TO USE

They say money makes the world go around and I say having the right money helps. You should always do your research about a country or island before going and find out about currency. The currency that is used in Abaco is BSD(Bahamian Dollar) or USD(American Dollar). So unless you are from America, you'd have to go to your bank and get a currency exchange. I also think it would be helpful to know that we have a Value added tax here that is 12%. When shopping you will pay this fee.

Moreover, it's best to keep some cash on you. Yes, we accept credit cards here but some places don't so it would be a smart idea to keep some cash on you in case you're caught off guard. Also sometimes ATMs can run out of money so that's another reason to bring along some. Many days I have been sorely disappointed by waiting in an ATM line only to find out that there isn't any money left. If that happens your only other option is to wait to get inside the bank to get to a teller. Be smart, come prepared.

Side note: It's also wise to let your bank know that you will be traveling. That way, if they see money being charged to your account in a foreign country they will know it's you and not some type of scam or fraud.

5. GOOGLE MAP CAN BE YOUR BEST FRIEND

If this is your first trip to Abaco, have no fear because Google maps are here. If you are a person that has a pet peeve of asking directions or is just straight up horrible at taking them, then a map is the way to go. My recommendation is Google maps. Google maps make it easy to know your location even and see where it is that you want to get to while giving an estimate of the time it should take and the different routes you can travel on. Even living in

Abaco as long as I have, there are places I still don't know by name and have to use google map's assistance for.

6. TRANSPORTATION

Unless you already have a prearranged ride to take you to your next destination, the most common way for a tourist to get around the island is by taxi. Taxis are usually outside the airport on standby so getting one is a fairly easy process. Just tell them where you want to go and make sure to ask the fare before you get in as many taxis don't have a meter. If you are okay with the price you can proceed to load up your luggage and be on your way. Also, the best way to pay is through cash. No credit cards.

There are also car rentals on the Island. If you most likely came to Abaco through the main airport in Marsh Harbour, there is a car rental at that very same airport as well. It makes things a little easier since you don't have to catch a taxi if you don't want to.

For those that choose to travel by car make sure to write down the names of the places you are trying to get to before you travel in case your phone battery dies. Even if you do end up having to ask for directions it's better than just being lost. I'd say if you're a solo female traveler ask another female for help. All the locals are pretty nice but just to stay on the safe side.

7. RED LIGHT GREEN LIGHT

Okay so you have the car and your map now the only thing left to wonder about is if there are hour-long traffic jams ahead. Traffic can be a real annoyance. If you were thinking about the traffic on Abaco, I have good news for you. There is little to no traffic here which is a blessing. I remember running late many days and being thankful the roads were practically clear. So if you are always running late at least you don't have traffic to further hold you back. Although not encouraged, if you're traveling in a tight time frame your chances of making it are pretty good.

If there is a case of extremely rare traffic, there are different routes to get to one area. As I stated earlier a map would be very helpful.

As far as road rage goes, we don't have many drivers like that in Abaco. If you are to face any blaring horns etc it would most likely be if you are at a stoplight that has turned green and you are taking too long to move. Other than that you shouldn't encounter anything even resembling road rage.

8. BE POLITE

There's an old saying here that goes " manners and respect will carry you around the world and bring you back safely". It's safe to say we as a people are big on respect. So much so that younger kids can get scolded for not showing respect to others, especially elders and it is normal here. As you're traveling you may see people saying good afternoon or morning etc and they are expecting you to say it back as common courtesy. It is also common to engage in a brief polite talk before making a request. A simple " Hello mam/sir how are you" would suffice. I remember walking along the street one day and passing an older woman without saying good afternoon. Big mistake. She did not hesitate to say " You can't speak eh? You see your elders and don't even say nothing. Yall too rude". To which I bit my tongue and apologized.

Abaconians are generally very easy-going and friendly people. As long as you aren't rude you will see that your experience is beyond pleasant. So smile and play nice.

9. WHY SO SERIOUS

In the essence of speaking on the attributes of the people from Abaco, it would not be right if I didn't find a way to mention humor. Bahamian people in general, share a common characteristic that is humor. From children straight up to adults we are always poking fun at something. Maybe it just runs in our blood. While I agree sometimes it can come off as taking it a bit too far to others that aren't used to our sense of humor, at the core, we are very light-hearted people and usually don't mean anything by it. So when coming here don't be so serious, have fun, and let your funny bone lead the way. If you are looking for a good laugh or to loosen up then it helps to surround yourself with people from Abaco.

10. LEARN SOME DIALECT/SLANG

The language spoken in Abaco is English however upon traveling here you will notice the locals have slang and dialect. Don't be afraid to ask what something means if you don't understand and definitely don't be afraid to try out some of the words. Abaconians will not bash you for trying, in fact, they might egg you on to try to use it in the spirit of good fun.

Some of the popular dialect words you may hear on your trip are :

- **Bui** (pronounced buh-yuh) has several meanings depending on how you say it. Most common meaning being hey you! , look at this or anything along the lines of asking for someone's attention. I use this often. To be honest this is probably the most used slang word.

- **Muddoe** (pronounced mud-dough) or **mudda sick** (pronounced mud-da-sick) meaning I can't believe this!

- **Conch** (pronounced con-k) is actually an animal here but locals refer to people that can't be taken seriously as a conch. It's like an inside joke.

- **Dem** (pronounced as dem) is referring to a group of people. Example: I'm going to dinner with Johnny dem. This just means that person is going out with Johnny and other people.

- **Tingum** (pronounced ting-um) is referring to a person, place, or thing that can't be remembered or recalled easily. An example would be " Did you get

- **Had go or sgern on (** pronounced as written) Both are different forms of saying " hello how are you? "

- **Bly me (** pronounced as written) This is a phrase that is popular among the younger locals and it simply means excuse my behavior or action. It is most often used after they have done or said something embarrassing.

11. CAY HOPPING

As I mentioned earlier, Abaco is divided into three main categories. This is Great Abaco, Little Abaco, and the Cays. Here in Abaco, we have an activity called Cay hopping. It is just as the name implies. It is where a visitor or local would travel (hop) from Cay to Cay enjoying the experiences each has to offer. This would be recommended for those of you coming for a longer period because these trips usually last a day or half a day each. Nonetheless, it's a great pastime but if you are looking to buy souvenirs it may be a little pricier than the mainland. I've always wanted to go Cay hopping but never got around to it. I have visited the Cays separately though. Either way the Cays are fun but for the maximum experience I'd recommend Cay hopping.

12. TRAVEL TO ELBOW CAY

Since we are talking about Cay hopping I will give a little insight on a few of the Cays. I'll start with one of the most popular Cays to visit in Abaco. The first being Elbow Cay; also known as Hope Town. I've enjoyed myself here and I can say a tour of this Cay is the way to go. Whether you go by golf car or foot you should take a look around. The most popular place on Elbow Cay to visit is the lighthouse. It was built in 1862 by the British Imperial lighthouse service and is still standing today. It is one of the last kerosene-fueled lighthouses in the world and stands one hundred and twenty feet high. Its vibrant red and white candy cane colors make it easy to spot from afar. Needless to say, it became a local landmark that is popular with tourists and locals alike. You are usually permitted to climb the long flight of stairs and look out the top. This is a way to get a good workout in as well! I remember my trip to Hope Town as if it was yesterday. I was cramping before I arrived halfway up the stairs...good times. The view overlooking the harbour made it worthwhile to me. Another local favorite is Tahiti Beach. This beach is secluded. There have been sightings of nurse sharks, giant starfish, sand dollars and other sea creatures. This is a great beach for animal lovers.

13. GUANA CAY

The second Cay I will mention is Guana Cay. It is modestly populated and peaceful. Once you get your ferry to Guana Cay you can rent a golf car and ride around the island. There are family-friendly activities like snorkeling, fishing and swimming. For the experts and daredevils among you, there is scuba diving, shark diving, or spearfishing. There is a scuba gear shop on the Cay called Dive Guana in case you don't plan on lugging your own scuba gear behind you. Not only can you buy gear but you can rent as well. They have a website called www.diveguana.com.

Accommodation wise there are rental homes, stores and restaurants available so you can stay overnight without a problem. One of the more popular restaurants is Grabbers which is a waterfront restaurant. It is a fun, tourist-friendly environment to visit and it makes for great photos too! Come on down, stand on the pier and take pictures during the sunset or sit on the beach and listen to a live band play. You will enjoy yourself at Grabbers.

14. NO NAME CAY

Before you start wondering- yes. The name of the Cay is No Name Cay. Despite not having a name, this Cay is very popular among the locals. They have a very lively atmosphere that is family friendly as well. The ferry ride there from the mainland is about twenty to thirty minutes.

At No Name Cay, you can swim with the pigs which should always make for an interesting story. Sometime people even call it piggyville because of the swimming pigs. You'll find it easiest to get in touch with Sunset Marina Tours. They will give you a private tour and take you to see the pigs. Depending on where you are staying you will have to get a ride to Treasure Cay to depart to get to No Name Cay.

There is also a restaurant and bar as well with music. The best time to go for the most lively experience is on a Sunday. That's when everyone comes out both local and tourist.

15. MOORE'S ISLAND

Now, I don't know what exactly to Call Moore's Island. I say this because although it has an island in the name, it is technically a Cay but we just don't call it that. Regardless, there are a few things to do there. Exploring the caves is one option. For those of you that love a good adventure you can trek through the caves pretending to be Dora. I'd recommend doing that with a group and with someone that knows their way around. These caves are also close to the landing strip bar and lounge, so when you're tired of playing caveman you can go enjoy civilization and have a cool drink.

Next would be the infamous blue hole. The young boys that grow up on the island can tell you about this. I'm not sure I would go swimming in it- mainly because I can't swim but it'd be a good selfie opportunity. If you do decide to dive, make sure you can swim and very well. Also, I wouldn't recommend going alone. The blue hole is also in close proximity to the landing strip bar and lounge so if you do fall in and have to hang on to the rocks someone should hear you screaming.

16. BEACH BASICS

Alrighty, we all know it was coming so let's get down to beach 101. There aren't any rules about going to the beaches but there are suggestions. The first being DO NOT FEED THE SEAGULLS. If you actually want to enjoy your beach day don't feed those pesky little creatures because they will not hesitate to turn on you. They will swoop down on your food supply ruthlessly and eat everything if you don't hide. Save yourself the trouble.

Second, if you get sunburnt easily, you should invest in an umbrella. As mentioned, the sun gets brutal at times. Thirdly, be prepared for a long drive. Abaco; the second largest island in The Bahamas, although still relatively small, can feel a bit long when traveling to the beaches. If you want to go to the best beaches you will have to travel a bit but it is worth the drive.

17. BEST BEACHES

Abaco has some of the prettiest beaches you will find. In fact, Treasure Cay beach was once voted one of the top 10 beaches in the world.I don't mean to brag (I do) but that's pretty honorable. When listing the beaches I will divide them into two categories, mainland (including little Abaco) and cays. Here are my top recommendations for beaches to visit.

Main Land
- Treasure Cay Beach (From Marsh Harbour to Treasure Cay is typically a thirty minute drive)
- Casuarina Beach (From Marsh Harbour to Casuarina Point is typically a forty minute drive)

Cays
- Town Beach(located on HopeTown /Elbow Cay)
- Tahiti Beach (located on HopeTown)
- Love Beach(located on Guana Cay)
- No Name Cay/Piggy Ville (located on No Name Cay)

18. WHERE TO STAY

Where you live definitely plays a part in the activities you partake in, the length of drives you have to make, and overall how many activities you can squeeze in during a given time. Regardless of which Cay or part of the land you want to live in, I will give recommendations for hotels, inn, and resorts. Hopefully it can make your decision making a little easier since you should have some clue of where to start. Also once again I will divide this into two categories.

Main Land

- Winding Bay- This is an upscale resort located on Cherokee.They feature top of the line amenities.
- Abaco Beach Resort- Also more on the upscale side, they are located on Marsh Harbour.
- Abaco Hillside Hotel- located along Great Abaco Highway, great for those who prefer smaller homely hotels.
- Calypso Hill- located along SC Bootle highway just before you arrive at Treasure

Cay, this place is very popular among the locals because of the atmosphere.

Cays
- FireFly Sunset Resort (located on Hope Town/Elbow Cay)
- Hope Town Inn and Marina (located on Hope Town/Elbow Cay)
- Turtle Hill Resort (located on Hope Town/Elbow Cay)
- Oceanfrontier Hideaway (located on Guana Cay)
- Grabbers Bed Bar and Grill (located on Guana Cay)
- Bluff House Beach Resort and Marina (located on Green Turtle Cay)

19. WHERE TO EAT

Who doesn't love a good meal? All locals can agree Island food is a delicacy. We even have food unique to us, but I'm jumping the gun here. Let's start with places to get the food.

Main Land

- Colors by the Sea- This is a sit-down open restaurant that is on the waterfront (hence the name). There is a bar and the prices are reasonable. Their typical hours of operation are eleven am to nine pm. I love going here because I love their loaded potatoes. Locals typically dress casually when eating here.

- Lovely's Delight - This is a takeout place located in Marsh Harbour near the airport. The prices are reasonable as well and they make a mean burger. They are quite large so unless you have a super appetite one burger can share between two people.

- Sheva's Take Out- Another takeout place with very reasonable prices. One of the least expensive places to eat from and the food is good too. They are located in Murphy Town. I go to Sheva'sTake out so often they probably know my order by heart.

- Pete's Pub and Gallery- Pete's Pub is a beach restaurant and sculpture foundry. Prices are leaning toward the expensive side.

- Trixie's- This is a family- friendly, dine-in restaurant that has a deck on the outside with a bar. Their prices are okay, nothing too expensive but not exactly cheap. I've eaten here on multiple occasions and I think the food is good. I'd recommend it.

- Three guys - This is a takeout place for just chicken and fries located in Murphy Town. This is a place the locals definitely go to often. Everything is under ten bucks. Next to it there is normally a local woman who makes conch Fritters. TRY THEM. I don't normally eat conch fritters but when I do it's only from her.

- Sandpiper inn- This is a hotel located in Schooner Bay that is open for takeout and outdoor dining. Non-hotel guests are welcome for dinner Thursday through Sunday, with reservations. You can reach them through email info@sandpiperabaco.com

Cays
- Grabbers - This is a beachfront restaurant that features an open bar. They are located in Guana Cay.
- On Da Beach Bar and Restaurant- This is also another beachfront restaurant and bar that is located on Hope Town. They have live music from a DJ on Friday's.

- Bluff House- This is a dine-in restaurant located on Green Turtle Cay.

20. FOOD

We have finally arrived at that part of the lesson where we get to talk about delicious, mouth watering food. Now be prepared to immerse yourself in our cultured foods. If you aren't already familiar with The Bahamas then I may mention a few foods that sound interesting, but don't be afraid to test out your taste buds with Abaconian cuisine. Ps, you should know that we are big on seafood. Here are some of the best local foods to try out.

- Conch Fritters - typically served as an appetizer, this snack is pieces of conch mixed in a flour-based batter then fried. It is served with a sauce mixture to dip the fritters in.
- Cracked Conch - This meal is most commonly served with fries or rice. It is a bruised conch dipped in an egg wash and fried down.
- Conch Salad - One of my personal favorites, this is raw conch- stay with me, cleaned, cut into bite-sized pieces, doused with lime, and

served with tomatoes and onions. It may sound scary but I can vouch that it is DELICIOUS.

- Pigeon Peas and Rice - Commonly served as part of your Sunday meal, each household spices theirs up a little differently but most times very tasty.
- Souse - Mainly served as a breakfast food, every local knows about souse. We have different variations of souse like souse chicken, hog souse, etc… It is usually served with Johnny bread.
- Stew fish - This is one of the more popular stews among the locals, specifically the older ones. It has been around a while and is commonly eaten with freshly baked bread.
- Minced Crawfish- This is shredded crawfish in a tomato paste based sauce. This is delicious. Every single time I eat this I clean my plate.Highly recommended.

21. DRINKS

Can't have you eating food with nothing to wash it down with, so now I'll tell you about some Abaconian drinks that the locals love. I will separate

the drinks from kid-friendly to not-so-kid-friendly.
Hint Hint.

Kid-Friendly
- Vitamalt- I personally love this drink. It's a tangy thick kind of drink that's not necessarily sweet but still tastes good. Some locals add cream to theirs.
- Goombay Soda (produced in The Bahamas) - A sweet drink I'm sure the kids will love.
- Fruit punch- This drink is actually similar to a Bahama Mama. The main difference is that this one is non - alcoholic.

Adult Drinks
- Bahama Mama - This is flavored rum infused with orange juice,pineapple juice and grenadine syrup.
- Bushwacker- this is more like a milkshake mixed with kahlua and creme and cacao
- Goombay Smash (Originated on Guana Cay)- is also another rum mixture that is on the sweeter side.
- Gully Wash (also known as sky juice)- is fitting for an island drink. This is coconut water, condensed milk and gin.

22. DESSERTS

If you're anything like me then you have a real sweet tooth or as we say in Abaco " Ya mouth too sweet ". We have many desserts and cakes etc. Some of the popular desserts include:

- Guava Duff- a very sweet cake infused with guava and drizzled with a dressing. (Only for the sweetest of tooth's.)
- Rum cake - a cake with rum inside; what else could be said.
- Pineapple Upside Down cake- My favorite of all cakes. It is called this because the cake is essentially upside down with the pineapple slices underneath.(For those with good taste)
- Potato bread - definitely preferred by the oldest generation alive, this is a bread made with sweet potatoes as the main ingredient. I have tried to force this one down before but I'm personally not a big fan. Despite my distaste for this bread, you should try it out for yourself. I won't judge you.

Less popular is benny cake, which is eaten at any time...if you're hungry enough.

23. TIPPING

In our restaurants, the gratuity is calculated as percentages and you get to pick which percentage you want to tip your waiter. In many cases, it is not mandatory to tip the waiter however at a few restaurants it is. Mandatory or not, we locals just do it to show appreciation.

24. WHAT NOT TO EAT

There aren't many things you shouldn't eat here however the locals love to take a gamble eating a particular fish that is not exactly safe to eat. Barracuda. The local men especially love to test their immune systems by eating this. Not every barracuda is poisoned but the chance of getting a bad one is high seeing that they are known to eat metal, watches, and other shiny objects. I have been told it tastes great, however, the potential food poisoning turned me off. I've recently even had a few family members that ate it and got terrible food poisoning and had to be transported to the doctor. If you choose to test it out anyway then may the force be with you.

In addition, you can't eat or catch a sea turtle. It is an illegal offense to do so.

25. SUNDAY AS A LOCAL

Most locals have fallen into a routine for Sundays. The typical Sunday as a local involves going to church, cooking a big Sunday meal, binge-watching shows, preparing for work the next day, and rest, lots of rest. We have others that like to spend that time with friends, go out for brunch or more popularly go to the cays. Whichever suits you best. For those of you that wouldn't mind attending church, I will name a few churches to visit.

- Zion Baptist cathedral (located in Murphy Town)
- Bethany Gospel Chapel (located in Murphy Town)
- Zion Baptist (located in FoxTown)
- St James Methodist Church (located in Hope Town/Elbow Cay)

26. NIGHT LIFE

Okay night owls, it's finally your turn. Whether it's clubs or just a bar for a drink I will name the most popular places to be at night. These are a few of my recommendations.

- Pete's Pub and Gallery- This is a bar and art Gallery.
- Nardo's- Bar
- Cat 5 - A restaurant and bar.
- Waveside Bar - This is a waterfront bar. They have pool tournaments and feature inside and outside seating.
- Grabbers- This is a waterfront bar and restaurant. The bar is opened up in a cabana type of style.
- SunDowners- This is a bar on Green turtle Cay that has karaoke on Mondays. This is for the more subtle night out.
- Floating Bar- This bar, located in Sandy Point is suspended on water. It is a fun place to get a drink and hang with the locals.

27. GO SAILING

It's known that Abaco is the boatman's island out of all islands in The Bahamas. This is primarily because of Man O War Cay where boats are built. The locals there have been boat-building for many years.

In the spirit of boats, I encourage you to go ahead and set sail on the high sea. Captain Bruce is popular among the captains for his day sailing trips. It would be fun for kids, teens, and adults. They also offer other activities such as kayaking, snorkeling, paddleboarding, and fishing. I tried fishing but I'm not very good because I'm terrified of live fish jumping around out of water

Fun fact about Man O War Cay: They used to be one of the only " dry" places in The Bahamas. This means they didn't sell or permit alcohol on Man O War.

Additionally on another Cay called green turtle cay there is a place called Lincoln Park where they will give you bait and allow you to feed the stingrays and sharks there. They also do bonfires where they roast food. It would be a great event for the whole family to attend.

28. LUCAYAN NATURE TOURS

Calling all birdwatchers, plant lovers, or just nature lovers in general. This one's for you. Nature is a beautiful thing so you should enjoy it and what better way than with a tour from Reginald. He is very knowledgeable about flora and fauna. A tour from him would be a great experience to learn about the history of our Island and see the hidden treasures Abaco has to offer. Reginald will pick you up and drop you back at your hotel after the tour. A tour can last a full day or less depending on what you decide. Go as a group, a couple, or solo but don't miss out! Get in contact with him and book a tour based on your interests in nature. You can reach him at oudi14@hotmail.com. Ps ask to see the Abaco parrots.

29. PICTURES TO TAKE

It's no doubt you will want to photograph the sites you see on your trip so I will help you with that too. A few photogenic sites are:

- The beaches of course (Treasure Cay beach is the most beautiful in my humble opinion)
- The Parrot Statue which is located in Marsh Harbour near the airport.
- The striped Lighthouse that is located in Hope Town.
- Blue Hole which is located on Moore's Island.
- Abaco Parrots - If you choose to book a nature tour you will see these birds along the way.
- Sculptures at Pete's Pub and gallery

30. DISNEY CRUISE

Even if you don't go to Abaco directly you can still make a stop via cruise. Disney has a cruise that goes to Castaway Cay, Abaco. It's a little Cay off of Great Abaco. If you're looking for something for the kids then that may be the perfect trip. There are lots of activities for everyone like parasailing, tetherball, volleyball, waterslides, etc. The island also features a teen hideout for teens ages 14-17. Another feature is an adult beach with massage cabanas. Finally, it features a place called In Da Shade which has ping pong tables, basketball, etc. The best part is that they have supervisors so tweens can hang out without their parent's supervision. Parents will be able to lay back and relax without worrying.

31. GOLF COURSE

For those of you with refined taste, come on down to Treasure Cay's golf course.This course was voted "The #1 Golf Course in the Bahamas" by Golf Digest. From beginner to pro you will have fun golfing on the course. If you are a single looking in need of a partner they will help you find one. To reach their email [TreasureCay.com/golf].

There is also another option of golfing on Winding bay however you would have to have a membership there to enjoy that particular golf course. This course features a practice facility that opened in 2016. Here, you can practice double end range as well as short games. If you love golfing then definitely check one of those out. You can reach The Abaco club on winding bay at their email info@theabacoclub.com.

32. TAKE HOME A SOUVENIR

What better way to remember your Abaco experience than a souvenir. There are souvenir shops to buy little articles like Albury's Sail Shop located in Man O War Cay where they sell bags, hats, pots, and bowls, etc. An additional souvenir store is Joe's Studio which is also in Man O War Cay. At this store you can get handcrafted model boats and sailing dinghies made from Abaco hardwood. If you can't make it to any of those stores, then you can just take back a Bahamian bill as a souvenir. Bahamian money is very colorful and vibrant and would make a nice little article to keep as a reminder of your trip to Abaco.

33. SOLO TRAVELER TRIPS

Whether female or male if you are a solo traveler there are a few tips I will give you when traveling.

The first tip is to stick to public places. Sure Abaco is relatively safe but you never want to be too careful when traveling alone. Avoid places with little to no people, especially during nighttime.

In relevance to the first, this tip would be to check in with a friend. Stay in touch. Even if there is no cause for concern, a daily check-in could be beneficial in the long run. In the same vein stay observant. Don't make yourself seem like a tourist, try to fit in and do what the locals do. Eat where we eat and avoid too many 'tourist-y' places. Don't dress in a way that screams ' Hey i'm not from here', locals dress casually. Jeans and tshirts is everyday wear here unless we go to dinner or church.

34. TIPS 2.0

Oftentimes when traveling we love to wear our shiniest piece of jewelry and carry around large bags thinking the best. As I mentioned Abaco is pretty safe, I've lived here for over twenty years and nothing has ever happened to me even once however I don't let it stop me from using my street smarts. When traveling try to leave valuables at home if not absolutely necessary to bring. Don't make yourself a target.

35. HOPE FOR THE BEST AND PREPARE FOR THE WORST

I'm sure as you plan your trip you have expectations for it to be perfect. Well, drop them. There aren't many people that can come back from a trip saying everything went exactly according to plan. We all know mishaps can happen to even the most well-organized of us so expect at least one thing to go wrong. That way if something does happen you won't lose your cool. You can never be in control of everything but you can prepare and when that fails just hope. Chances are things won't be half as bad as you make them out to be in your mind.

36. ISLAND QUIRKS

The islands of the Bahamas are very similar in the characteristics and traits of the people, however, there are some traits only particular islands have. For example, until I stayed in Nassau for a while recently, I never knew that only Abaconians took eating Mahatma rice so seriously. Sure it sounds funny because it's just a brand of rice but it's basically one of the only rice brands we eat in Abaco and definitely the most preferred. I struggled with having to eat parboiled rice---not that it was bad but I wasn't used to eating it.Another island quirk I just recently found about is sausage souse. Now if you know about souse the last thing we do is put sausage in it. This is more of a little Abaco quirk as it is popular there.

37. CONCH SALAD WITH MAYO?

Now I know you're probably thinking conch salad sounds intimidating as it is and now we're adding something new to the mix. Yes, in Abaco we sometimes add mayo to our conch salad. I don't typically do it but it's commonly done here. People of other islands in The Bahamas sometimes even poke fun at us for eating it that way, to which I say to each his own. Personally, I just think they're jealous that we came up with the idea first.

38. VISITING ON NEW YEARS EVE

New Year's Eve is a time to celebrate going forward into another year, to be surrounded by those close to you. While we may not be able to watch the ball drop, we do have a tradition here. Typically speaking, we are religious people so it may not come as a surprise that in Abaco we typically have watch night services; which is just a church service on December 31 around 9/10 to 12 o'clock January 1st. We like to bring in the new year by giving thanks to God for our lives and being grateful. However, in every culture, some people do things differently so you may find some cars on the roads or maybe even a party happening. If you were to travel here during this time that's what would typically occur.

39. VISITING DURING HOLIDAYS- CHRISTMAS

On Christmas day you can expect another big meal. We lay it all out on the table- literally. Ham, turkey, peas and rice, sides, and an array of desserts.

People use this time to come together to spend time, open presents, and share memories and laughs. I'd say Christmas is the most celebrated holiday. Boxing day which is the next day after Christmas there is typically some sort of junkanoo rush. If you aren't familiar with Junkanoo it's like a festival or gathering where we play Bahamian music using goatskin drums, cowbells, trumpets, trombones, etc. Big, colorful, handmade costumes are worn. It is a very fun experience, especially for music-loving tourists.

Fun fact: Boxing day stems from when servants, tradespeople, and the poor traditionally were presented with gifts.

40. VISITING DURING HOLIDAYS- INDEPENDENCE DAY

The final Holiday I will discuss is the most important one. Independence Day. July 10th is a joyous day for Abaconians. On this day you will most likely see parties happening, cars with Bahamian flags waving on the road, sometimes motorcades, etc. It is a day of enjoying Bahamian foods and music and just the culture in general. For those that want to get a taste of our culture, then is the best time to travel to Abaco.

41. BUSIEST AND SLOWEST MONTHS

Upon living here and observing, I can come to a close conclusion that the busiest months to visit Abaco are normally from March to July. During summer breaks everyone wants to go to the beach. We even have spring breakers coming in and it can get pretty hectic. The slowest months are around September and October. This is probably because it's when school is reopening for most.

42. GENERAL EXPENSES

Now that you know where to go, what to do, what to eat, drink, and all that good stuff, it's time to get down to expenses. Honestly speaking, I'd say the expense for a trip to Abaco depends on where you choose to stay. It's one of those deciding factors where you have to weigh the good and bad of each option. On one hand, staying on the mainland is cheaper than living on one of the Cays, however, if you plan on traveling to the Cays frequently for the activities, the prices for tickets will add up in the long run. Then on the other hand staying on the Cays can help you save on ferry tickets but the prices for food and overall expenses are drastically different than the mainland.

43. ABACONIAN FESTIVALS/ LOCAL GAMES

Here in Abaco, we have a few festivals the locals absolutely love. The first is something we call homecoming. More than one settlement has a homecoming event. There is one in little Abaco, Sandy Point(which is at the opposite end of the mainland) and Moore's Island. For the party goers homecoming is a dream. During homecoming us locals share classic Bahamian dishes, have entertainment such as dj's and have a good time socializing among themselves. This is a family friendly event so you can bring the kids along. Children normally would play on the beaches, oftentimes with the older kids jumping from the dock and swimming around for fun.

Next we have an adult event called CheeseBurger in paradise. Interesting choice for a name I know but it has nothing to do with cheeseburgers ironically. Everyone gathers in a central area on party boats blasting music, drinking, dancing and just having fun with friends. This is the perfect time to break out those swimsuits and show off that beach body! This party usually happens in the waters around fiddle Cay.

Moving along to local games there is dominoes, shooting dice, shooting marbles etc... Lately some of those games have slowly been forgotten. All except one.

In my opinion, Dominoes will always be a favorite in Abaconian culture. In fact, the last time I had a family event they were playing dominoes. It's just basically a matching numbers game. Abaconian men sometimes gamble over a game of dominoes. They tend to get excited while playing. If you ever get a chance to observe a game you may be a little taken aback at the shouting, slamming the game pieces down and even name calling. I promise you they don't take it to heart, it's just how they play.

After a game they will gather over beers laughing and smiling again as if nothing ever happened.

44. FOOD/HOTELS AND LIVING ACCOMMODATIONS

If you plan on doing some shopping you should be forewarned that it's more expensive to eat healthily. So bring along a few extra bucks for food if you have a strict diet to stay on.

Now when it comes to living accommodations I'm going to be blunt here. A common hotel price is around 200-300$ a night. If you book with an AirBnB instead, you can get a steal. Air BnB's range from 150 to 250$ a night and in most cases, you get a whole apartment to yourself. I suppose living arrangements depend on what you are comfortable with. Most tourists like to stay at a hotel to be around other people but if you don't mind being alone then an AirBnB is for you.

45. CAR RENTALS

The car rentals in Abaco are reasonable. As much as I would like to give you an exact quote I can't because prices sometimes vary on what type of car, model, etc. However, I will give you a few of the car rentals names:

- Barefoot Car Rentals (located Marsh Harbour)
- Bargain Car Rental (located Marsh Harbour)
- Sg Car Rental (located at Leonard Thompson Airport, Marsh Harbour)

46. MORE INFORMATION

In the spirit of cars, it is crucial to know that we drive on the left side of the road in Abaco. I know in other countries it may be the right but not here. So if you don't want to end up in a high-speed chase or swerving for your life, stick to the left-hand side. I mean what are you going to tell the police if they pull you over and see this book in the car with me specifically telling you to stay on the left-hand side. Looks bad right? Moreover, when it comes to driving in Abaco you will need an international driving permit. United Kingdom and American drivers licenses are valid in Abaco.

47. DON'T FORGET TO RELAX

I know this is a lot of information and that you want your trip to go as smoothly as possible but don't forget to stop and relax. The main reason for your trip is most likely relaxation so don't leave it out. Unwind, go for a walk, sit by the ocean but don't stress yourself with everything that's going on. Take a breather. Be patient. Bury your feet in the sand….or not because it's probably over a hundred degrees.

48. LESSONS

Although a trip to Abaco is all in good fun that doesn't mean you can't have a learning experience. For me, living in Abaco taught me that in life it's the little things that matter. Just to be able to live and enjoy the sun, the ocean, and nature in itself is a gift. Sure there are many things I can complain about but why should I spend my time grumbling about what isn't instead of being grateful for what is.

Besides a moral lesson, you can learn about another culture other than yours. You may find similarities or you may have a complete culture shock. You will learn to respect opinions that differ from your own.Moreover, you will learn something new that you can go back home and share with your family and friends.

You will also learn the importance of being family oriented.

49. WHY YOU SHOULD VISIT

Overall the reasons you should take a trip to Abaco are the beaches, the friendly people, the array of activities to partake in and learn about our island culture and way of life. The atmosphere is just all-around peaceful and one that makes it easy to relax. In addition, a trip to Abaco is family-friendly in that there is an activity for everyone to do. You have an opportunity to try new things like island hopping and going to some of the best local parties and events.

50. LAST BUT NOT LEAST

Bring a first aid kit. Abaco is a place that has lots of rocks and some are exceptionally sharp. While you don't have to expect a blood bath you should bring along a first aid kit. Accidents happen and kids are clumsy.

Bonus tip - In Abaco there are only two mobile service providers which are ALIV and BTC. That said if you need to call you would have to use the hotel's internet or purchase an international plan.

Bonus tip- Be prepared for outdoor activities. In Abaco, there aren't movie theaters, bowling alleys, amusement parks, etc. Most activities are done outdoors so you should come prepared for that. Also be prepared to go boating, if you are a person that gets seasick then I recommend that you do other activities. You can still enjoy the beach just not at the risk of losing your lunch.

Bonus tip- Places to shop for food- The main food stores in Abaco are Maxwell's Supermarket, Abaco Groceries, and Quality Meats And Spices. A place to shop for clothes would be Island Girl Boutique. All places are located in Marsh Harbour.

Bonus tip- Don't over-plan your days. Plan maybe one to three activities for a day and let the rest fill itself in. Leave a little room to be spontaneous. Remember that traveling is more about the journey. You'd be surprised, the days you will just wing it can be some of the most exciting ones.

Bonus tip- Get travel insurance. You can never possibly know what surprises may come up during your trip whether good or bad. Travel insurance protects you in case you get sick or injured, robbed, the flight is canceled, etc. It is a smart investment to make.

Bonus tip- Make a copy of your passport photo and keep the original in a safe place. It may sound silly but you never know when you may need it so having those photos on hand definitely helps. If you easily lose things this is a great idea for you.

Bonus tip- Make friends with the locals. When going to visit a place the best thing to do is try to make friends with the locals. Be friendly but still cautious. Locals can help give you some of the best places for food,to hang out etc. You never know, maybe you will make a lifelong friend. I'd also say to be open minded when speaking to locals. If you're having a discussion and you don't agree with their opinion, still listen. Don't just assume your right, hear the other person out because you will gain insight to the way they think and live. Other people have different experiences and opinions than you and that's okay.

Bonus tip- Invest in a good camera. Unless you plan on filling up your phone's memory space with pictures you should invest in a quality camera. You don't want your pictures to look like a caveman took them on a rock phone while running away from a bear! Good camera quality will have you proud to show off your photos.

Bonus tip- Drone rules. There are some rules you have to follow if you want to fly a drone. The main one is that your drone needs to be registered. You can register here: https://caabahamas.com/drone-registration/
You can't fly within fifty feet of a person that is not associated with your drone's operation. You can't

fly within five nautical miles of an airport. I believe you will find the list on this website helpful: https://uavcoach.com/drone-laws-in-the-bahamas/

Bonus tip- Just so you know, in The Bahamas we have a hurricane season which is from June to November. Not every year we receive hurricanes but it is important to know that if you travel to Abaco around this time there is a possibility. In any event, it's good to have some type of plan for that if you travel during this time.

TOP REASONS TO BOOK THIS TRIP

Beaches: Here, you will see and enjoy some of the most pristine and beautiful beaches with clear waters.

Culture: You get to have a taste of our culture through foods, music, and our general way of life.

Family Friendly: The people are easygoing, friendly and funny. The places in Abaco offer activities for adults, teens and kids. No one will be left out.

Food: The food is delicious and different. You get to try new foods and even carry back home recipes.

With these tips and knowledge I've shared, you should be well on your way to being greater than a tourist.

TRIVIA QUESTIONS

1. What settlement in Abaco is known for its boat building?
2. What was the name of Abaco before 1783?
3. How many miles long is Abaco?
4. Who were the first known inhabitants of Abaco?
5. What tourist attraction is in Hope Town that has been dated from the 19th century?
6. Which Abaconian drink originated on Guana Cay?
7. In which year did the Abacos try to withdraw from The Bahamas as an independent country with London?
8. Which bird is Abaco known for?
9. Which major Hurricane struck Abaco in 2019?
10. Which well known Company issued an article about the blue holes in Abaco?

ANSWERS

1. Man O War
2. Carleton Point
3. 3. 120 miles long
4. The Lucayans
5. The red and white striped lighthouse
6. Goombay Smash
7. 1960
8. The Abaco Parrot
9. Hurricane Dorian
10. National Geographic

Travel map link I believe will be helpful:

https://abacoestateservices.com/abaco-map.html

PACKING AND PLANNING TIPS

A Week before Leaving

- Arrange for someone to take care of pets and water plants.

- Email and Print important Documents.

- Get Visa and vaccines if needed.

- Check for travel warnings.

- Stop mail and newspaper.

- Notify Credit Card companies where you are going.

- Passports and photo identification is up to date.

- Pay bills.

- Copy important items and download travel Apps.

- Start collecting small bills for tips.

- Have post office hold mail while you are away.

- Check weather for the week.

- Car inspected, oil is changed, and tires have the correct pressure.

- Check airline luggage restrictions.

- Download Apps needed for your trip.

69

Right Before Leaving

- Contact bank and credit cards to tell them your location.

- Clean out refrigerator.

- Empty garbage cans.

- Lock windows.

- Make sure you have the proper identification with you.

- Bring cash for tips.

- Remember travel documents.

- Lock door behind you.

- Remember wallet.

- Unplug items in house and pack chargers.

- Change your thermostat settings.

- Charge electronics, and prepare camera memory cards.

READ OTHER
GREATER THAN A TOURIST
BOOKS

Greater Than a Tourist- California: 50 Travel Tips from Locals

Greater Than a Tourist- Salem Massachusetts USA50 Travel Tips from a Local by Danielle Lasher

Greater Than a Tourist United States: 50 Travel Tips from Locals

Greater Than a Tourist- St. Croix US Birgin Islands USA: 50 Travel Tips from a Local by Tracy Birdsall

Greater Than a Tourist- Montana: 50 Travel Tips from a Local by Laurie White

Children's Book: Charlie the Cavalier Travels the World by Lisa Rusczyk Ed. D.

> TOURIST

Follow us on Instagram for beautiful travel images:
http://Instagram.com/GreaterThanATourist

Follow *Greater Than a Tourist* on Amazon.

CZYKPublishing.com

> TOURIST

At *Greater Than a Tourist*, we love to share travel tips with you. How did we do? What guidance do you have for how we can give you better advice for your next trip? Please send your feedback to GreaterThanaTourist@gmail.com as we continue to improve the series. We appreciate your constructive feedback. Thank you.

METRIC CONVERSIONS

TEMPERATURE

110° F — — 40° C
100° F —
90° F — — 30° C
80° F —
70° F — — 20° C
60° F —
50° F — — 10° C
40° F —
32° F — — 0° C
20° F —
— -10° C
10° F —
0° F — — -18° C
-10° F —
-20° F — — -30° C

To convert F to C:

Subtract 32, and then multiply by 5/9 or .5555.

To Convert C to F:

Multiply by 1.8 and then add 32.

32F = 0C

LIQUID VOLUME

To Convert:................Multiply by
U.S. Gallons to Liters................ 3.8
U.S. Liters to Gallons 26
Imperial Gallons to U.S. Gallons 1.2
Imperial Gallons to Liters....... 4.55
Liters to Imperial Gallons 22
1 Liter = .26 U.S. Gallon
1 U.S. Gallon = 3.8 Liters

DISTANCE

To convert ....Multiply by
Inches to Centimeters 2.54
Centimeters to Inches 39
Feet to Meters...................... .3
Meters to Feet 3.28
Yards to Meters 91
Meters to Yards 1.09
Miles to Kilometers 1.61
Kilometers to Miles............ .62
1 Mile = 1.6 km
1 km = .62 Miles

WEIGHT

1 Ounce = .28 Grams
1 Pound = .4555 Kilograms
1 Gram = .04 Ounce
1 Kilogram = 2.2 Pounds

TRAVEL QUESTIONS

- Do you bring presents home to family or friends after a vacation?

- Do you get motion sick?

- Do you have a favorite billboard?

- Do you know what to do if there is a flat tire?

- Do you like a sun roof open?

- Do you like to eat in the car?

- Do you like to wear sun glasses in the car?

- Do you like toppings on your ice cream?

- Do you use public bathrooms?

- Did you bring a cell phone and does it have power?

- Do you have a form of identification with you?

- Have you ever been pulled over by a cop?

- Have you ever given money to a stranger on a road trip?

- Have you ever taken a road trip with animals?

- Have you ever gone on a vacation alone?

- Have you ever run out of gas?

- If you could move to any place in the world, where would it be?

- If you could travel anywhere in the world, where would you travel?

- If you could travel in any vehicle, which one would it be?

- If you had three things to wish for from a magic genie, what would they be?

- If you have a driver's license, how many times did it take you to pass the test?

- What are you the most afraid of on vacation?

- What do you want to get away from the most when you are on vacation?

- What foods smell bad to you?

- What item do you bring on ever trip with you away from home?

- What makes you sleepy?

- What song would you love to hear on the radio when you're cruising on the highway?

- What travel job would you want the least?

- What will you miss most while you are away from home?

- What is something you always wanted to try?

- What is the best road side attraction that you ever saw?

- What is the farthest distance you ever biked?

- What is the farthest distance you ever walked?

- What is the weirdest thing you needed to buy while on vacation?

- What is your favorite candy?

- What is your favorite color car?

- What is your favorite family vacation?

- What is your favorite food?

- What is your favorite gas station drink or food?

- What is your favorite license plate design?

- What is your favorite restaurant?

- What is your favorite smell?

- What is your favorite song?

- What is your favorite sound that nature makes?

- What is your favorite thing to bring home from a vacation?

- What is your favorite vacation with friends?

- What is your favorite way to relax?

- Where is the farthest place you ever traveled in a car?

- Where is the farthest place you ever went North, South, East and West?

- Where is your favorite place in the world?

- Who is your favorite singer?

- Who taught you how to drive?

- Who will you miss the most while you are away?

- Who if the first person you will contact when you get to your destination?

- Who brought you on your first vacation?

- Who likes to travel the most in your life?

- Would you rather be hot or cold?

- Would you rather drive above, below, or at the speed limited?

- Would you rather drive on a highway or a back road?

- Would you rather go on a train or a boat?

- Would you rather go to the beach or the woods?

TRAVEL BUCKET LIST

1.

2.

3.

4.

5.

6.

7.

8.

9.

10.

NOTES

>TOURIST

Made in the USA
Monee, IL
15 December 2023